DESTINY

WHEN LIFE MAKES

NO SENSE

UNDERSTANDING YOUR LEAH SEASON

PAUL BARRATT

Scripture quotations marked (NASB) are taken from the New American Standard Bible®, Copyright © 1960, 1962, 1963, 1968, 1971, 1972, 1973,1975, 1977, 1995 by The Lockman Foundation Used by permission. (www.Lockman.org)

Scripture quotations marked (NIV) are taken from the Holy Bible, New International Version®, NIV®. Copyright © 1973, 1978, 1984, 2011 by Biblica, Inc.™ Used by permission of Zondervan. All rights reserved worldwide.

Scripture quotations marked (NKJV) are taken from the New King James Version®. Copyright © 1982 by Thomas Nelson, Inc. Used by permission. All rights reserved.

Scripture taken from The Message. Copyright © 1993, 1994, 1995, 1996, 2000, 2001, 2002. Used by permission of NavPress Publishing Group.

Trust the process,

May you find purpose through seasons of uncertainty.

Paul

THIS BOOK IS DEDICATED TO THOSE IN PURSUIT OF PURPOSE AND DESTINY.

YOU ARE DIFFERENT,

YOU ARE DETERMINED,

YOU ARE UNIQUE.

CONTENTS

INTRODUCTION

Have you ever found yourself in the midst of a place where nothing seems to make sense anymore? Your daily routine is just that–a routine. You attempt to make strides in your life in accordance with the desires and passions you believe God placed within your heart. Yet there always seems to be another obstacle, another mountain, another hindrance, another test, and another challenge. But deep down you know there is more, much more, if you could just make sense out of what was going on in your life right now.

Some people have well-paying jobs, live in a nice house and have a couple of children but they're not fulfilled. Some find themselves in less fortunate situations, struggling financially, living paycheck-to-paycheck, and praying there are no surprise expenses at the end of the week. Others face divorce, heartache, tragedy, broken families, and abuse. We all have a story to tell and way too often we become so focused on ourselves, and distracted by the circumstances around us, that we miss the bigger picture of what really is taking place and what it is that God has called us to do. The world is in desperate need of what the Lord has designed for you and I to accomplish.

Have you ever come across someone with a "real" problem and felt like yours pales in comparison? When this happens reality shows up and slaps us all in the face. The truth is that someone somewhere is always dealing with something bigger, more tragic and more heart-wrenching than we are, and it takes a rude awakening for us to realize how blessed we truly are. At that point our focus shifts to another realm and maybe, just maybe, we get a glimpse of a future that is brighter and more fulfilling. This positions us to embrace a destiny that not only makes a difference in our own lives but in the lives of many others.

Sunday arrives and we put on our best church clothes and our Christian smiles, but deep down many of us are imploding, hurting and feeling like we have no rational answers for our current conditions. We constantly check ourselves and ask God to examine us, thinking, "Somehow I must have done something wrong that has put me in this place." The cycle then begins to repeat itself, over and over again; silence, emptiness, struggles, laughter, tears, peace, turmoil, hope and joy, all wrapped up into one mess of a life that we can't quite seem to figure out. We know that if it were not for God, we would have lost our minds years ago. Thankfully, there is more to the story, much more.

Each of us has a specific journey from God that, when embraced, takes us into seasons that redefine our lives and equip us for the very purpose we were designed. It's not always easy and we are sometimes pulled into what can feel like a raging battle, but ultimately the end result is our destiny.

There are individuals and churches that recognize and understand this journey and are equipped to help you navigate through it. However, there are some that do not. Some will attempt to impose their visions upon your life, in an effort to build their own empires, while neglecting the fact that you have an individual destiny of your own to fulfill. And while I completely believe in, and support, the vision of the local house, (because after all we are the Body of Christ) giving up your individual destiny for someone else's vision is not what God wants you to do.

Yet there are some people who see fulfilling their destiny as way too difficult. They decide against it, even when God has put His hand on their lives for a purpose. And others completely ignore their calling, in pursuit of worldly passions, and go to their graves with unfulfilled destiny. Some go it alone without counsel, guidance or spiritual covering and feel they are still in the perfect will of God; as they continue along the wrong path with blinders on simply because they refuse to ask for help.

And for those of us on the right track, we sometimes find ourselves unintentionally resisting the hand of God because our idea of what things should look like are far different than the way He intended them to be. Our reaction to certain situations causes us to fight, or so we think, against the principalities and powers of darkness, when in fact it is simply the hand of God moving us closer to our destiny. The pressures, confinement, and restrictions we face can often be tools that God uses to move us forward on to His path as He takes us off our own.

Please don't misunderstand me; there are times when we must stand and fight the enemy of our soul that attempts to rob, steal, and destroy our destinies. But there are seasons when we must correctly discern the very hand of God moving in our midst and not confuse it as an attack from the enemy. When nothing makes sense amidst all of the chaos and disappointment, there is a vein of purpose that is threaded throughout your circumstances that paints a portrait of your incredible journey in God, advancing you forward into His perfect will for your life.

This book will take you on a prophetic journey designed to bring clarity in the midst of uncertainty in your life. The goal is for you to see the unfolding purpose of each season God has ordained for you and your family. These seasons (although not always comfortable or ideal) are not designed to destroy you, but to shape and mold you into the specific purpose and destiny God has called you to fulfill.

The following chapters will appear all too familiar as you see yourself walking in Jacob's shoes and begin to witness the same struggles and frustrations as he once did. My hope is that you will begin to see the handprint of God's design in every situation and circumstance in your life, just as the diversity of events unfolded in Jacob's life that eventually launched him into his destiny.

I began writing this book in the midst of the darkest season of my life, holding on to the truth that was set before me, that 'He would never leave me or forsake me' in my hour of need. Many years have passed since then, and even though it was never clear to me as to the length of that particular season, I am blessed to tell you that I am now walking out part of my destiny.

Now, let's take a walk into DESTINY and Understanding Your Leah Season...

CHAPTER 1

REBEKAH'S CRY

If you are familiar with the life of Jacob you know he had plenty of highs and lows. He had an incredible ability to escape conflict, exhibit cunning moves, and lead a life full of intrigue. If we simply read his life story (Genesis 25–50) and take it at face value, we witness amazing events, historical facts, and an incredible move of God in one man's life. Jacob was a great patriarch and defender of the faith whose destiny would be to bare a nation unto God.

If we dig a little deeper, we find a hidden undercurrent that can easily be overlooked when we only focus on the surface of this story. Taking the time to allow God to reveal his Word though the unfolding events in Jacobs life presents a completely different picture. The same can be said for our own lives. It is possible that we would have a much better understanding of the dealings of God during specific times and seasons if we would only take the time to step back and see it from a different vantage point. When we do, we have the ability to gain a godly perspective of the events that are shaping our future through seasons of uncertainty.

Let us begin at the best place – the beginning. In Genesis 24, we learn that Abraham sent his chief servant to find a bride for his son, Isaac. Once the servant found her and made the request of her family to be a wife for Isaac, she was sent to marry him. Her name was Rebekah.

Before Rebekah left home, her family blessed her with a prophetic prayer: *"Our sister, may you increase to thousands upon thousands; may your offspring possess the cities of their enemies."* Gen. 24:60 (New International Version). Unbeknown to the bride, a decree was established over her life that would shape history as we know it today. She gave birth to a child who they called Jacob, who would in turn become the father of Judah, and that genealogy would eventually lead to Jesus the Messiah. However, Rebekah encountered a problem. She was barren, which led to humiliation and embarrassment for her and frustration and upset for her husband.

When we receive a word from the Lord over our lives and the direct opposite happens, we are often left believing one of two things: either, "I must accept the current prognosis," or "I must believe for the impossible." There is always a contradiction to the word, and even when we do not understand the depth or future intentions of that word, we must never allow ourselves to be robbed of it. Rebekah and Isaac chose the latter and after Isaac prayed for his wife, she conceived. But the fight didn't stop there.

Isaac prayed to the Lord on behalf of his wife, because she was childless. The Lord answered his prayer, and his wife Rebekah became pregnant. The babies jostled each other within her, and she said, "Why is this happening to me?" So she went to inquire of the Lord.

The Lord said to her. "Two nations are in your womb,
and two peoples from within you will be separated;
one people will be stronger than the other,
and the older will serve the younger." Gen. 25:21-23 (NIV)

Turmoil would be a good word to describe Rebekah's condition; pregnant with anticipation and uncomfortable beyond description. This natural picture illustrates the twists and turns we so often experience in our lives, where the birthing of what God has placed within us yearns to come forth, except we want it without all the pain and discomfort.

Having received their callings long before conception, the struggle the twin boys shared was evident, even to Rebekah. Destiny was resident within her womb, yet she did not have the understanding of the depth and purpose of what her sons' birth would represent.

WHY ME, LORD?

As we see in the passage above, Rebekah cried out to God, "Why is this happening to me?" (Genesis 25:22 NIV). The Message Bible translates her cry in this way: "If this is the way it's going to be, why go on living?" She had had enough. Rebekah's discomfort became a desperate cry for answers that resonated in the hallways of Heaven and into the throne of God. Two Nations (Jacob and Esau) were fighting for position and territorial dominion before they were ever born, and Rebekah felt this struggle deep within her womb.

You may have never been told this before, but for a Word to come to pass in your life first requires surgery. The uncomfortable and at times painful situations we endure in our lives are often the result of the Lord mercifully exposing our flaws by applying pressure to certain areas. This ultimately gets our attention. Sometimes these pressure points can be un-forgiveness, unhealthy relationships, addictions, sin and past hurts - which some of us deal with on a daily basis. But God sees you as a finished work, and we need to allow Him to refine us through seasons of change, so that His word can be fulfilled the way He intended it. The underlying struggle and the fierce unrelenting discomfort are no more than destiny, designed by God, pulling you into your future. Next time you encounter a difficult situation or season, take the time and see how it applies to the Word over your life and the changes that you have to personally make.

Too often we focus on how much it hurts and how much we are lacking, but that inevitably causes us to miss the bigger picture. Too many of us pull away from God in times of crisis rather than draw closer to Him. If we would crawl back up into Daddy's arms and hear his voice of comfort and reason, then the storms would subside, the waves would be still, and we would begin to hear his sweet voice once again, speaking into our lives.

I remember very clearly when our children were young, whenever they got hurt on the playground or one of their friends called them a bad name, they would always come running to us with tears in their eyes crying for help. We would patch them up, speak words of encouragement over them, and then pray for them to find peace and healing. Never once did they run away from us. In their eyes, mom and dad had the power to make all things better. That's the beauty in the innocence of a child. So why then, when things don't 'go our way' as adults, do we get upset with God? After all, He has all the answers and all the comfort we will ever need.

When Rebekah inquired of the Lord, she received an answer that "two nations" were in her womb. It was an answer to prayer for her, and the unveiling of what took place was far from what she expected. As we position ourselves to hear a word from God - whether it is a vision, dream, prophetic word or visitation - the word in itself has to come full-term. It operates in the background, orchestrating a time and season for release, moving you here and there as you navigate through life's journey. As with any word, there are always periods of waiting, and a need to understand the timing of God. It's not always fun to wait, but I know day by day I am drawing closer to my purpose and destiny in Him.

The unfortunate calamity that too often takes place is that some people supernaturally abort their destinies by not carrying their promises to full term, or worse yet, not even realizing they have a destiny to begin with. They feel the price is too great for them to bare, and they eventually settle into the status-quo of mediocrity and coast through life not understanding the gifts, talents and abilities they carry serve a greater purpose beyond their 9-5 job. It is a great tragedy to see people fall away from their destiny. If only they would have held on just a little while longer, approached life a little differently, explored other options and pierced the veil of opportunity, then their breakthrough was within arms reach.

Before we continue. It is important to remember that God is not a taskmaster and does not erase our names from the Lambs Book of Life if we chose to not fully embrace our destiny and fulfill our purpose here on Earth. He still loves us and He still died for all. I wanted to interject this statement here because I realize some of you may know people who have had a great call on their lives and decided to walk away from it, for whatever reason, but they still loved God and never gave up on Him, and God never stopped loving them. It really comes down to choices.

THE CHOICE IS YOURS

Make no mistake; choosing to fully serve God has a price attached to it. This we know, because we've heard preachers tell us there's a price, but we don't always fully comprehend what that involves, especially when we are in the midst of being shaken. And everybody's price is a little bit different than the next person. Part of that shaking requires a cutting away of the accumulated excess baggage in our lives, which I gave a few examples of earlier, and moving to a clearer understanding of the things of God. Choosing to release the "stuff" in our lives and taking a hold of God in a fresh way will propel you into your future designed by Him. There is more to your present circumstances than what you are seeing right now.

Rebekah was faced with a choice to either endure the uncomfortable season of carrying a promise, or hate her very existence and circumstance. She chose wisely but she also had to adjust her way of thinking about how she felt and redirect it to the promise she was carrying in her womb.

When the pressures and obstacles of life have attempted to close in around me, I have often asked myself the following question: Would I be willing to position myself for 30 years of instruction, preparation, and discipline, feeling invisible to those around me, to be powerfully used of God for just three years? Jesus knew the timing and preparation for his ministry. I'm not Jesus but if it took Him 30 years to walk into his divine purpose, why do we think we can reach ours in five or less? It takes time!

We have all wanted to throw in the towel and call it quits at some point, I don't know anyone who has never considered that. Jesus even asked of the Father if possible let this cup pass from Me. Some seasons can become agonizing in nature but God doesn't throw the towel in on us, He is long suffering and caring. If you have made mistakes and failed, He is merciful to forgive and forget. Get back on your feet, dust yourself off and get back in the saddle one more time and believe his word in Psalms 37:23 (New King James Version)

The steps of a good man are ordered by the Lord:
and he delighteth in his way.
Though he fall, he shall not be utterly cast down:
for the Lord upholdeth him with his hand

Rebekah probably felt much like you and I when faced with a difficult season - afraid of what tomorrow may bring, uncertain of what lies ahead, questioning everything and everyone. But jumping ship was not an option for Rebekah, and it doesn't have to be for you either. The only thing that kept her going was the word she had heard from the Lord and the promise she was about to birth.

The flesh can be a very powerful adversary when subjected to the enemy's lies. At times we can feel bombarded with a constant diatribe of negative words, but our spirit, refined and in tune with God is an impenetrable wall against the principalities and powers of darkness. The Lord's voice penetrates through the darkness giving our spirit priority over our flesh, which allows us to see a much clearer picture of what God is doing in and through us on a daily basis. Think on the Word of God and how many people throughout history have made it despite times of trial and tribulation; Daniel, Joseph, David, Esther, and the list goes on and on. They were men and women of God just like you and me who were called to do incredible things, but that didn't mean it was easy for them.

You are uniquely created and He has called you to fulfill a specific purpose. Don't give up!

CHAPTER 2

JACOB'S GRASP

God had spoken over Rebekah that her sons would represent two nations; one was to be stronger than the other and the older would serve the younger. Finally, Jacob and Esau emerge. The weight of the promise had come full-term and behold, the two nations were birthed.

Jacob came out of the womb grasping the heel of his brother, Esau, and ironically, would never let go until he got what he wanted.

As scripture unfolds, we see that Jacob ended up inheriting the birthright of the firstborn despite being born after Esau. You may be wondering why the Lord allowed Jacob to be born after Esau when he ended up with everything anyway. And even though scripture reveals that these things would happen, we have labeled Jacob as a deceiver and heel-grabber. Something doesn't seem to add up, does it? Was God expecting Jacob to be the great deceiver and manipulator, or was there something happening in the background that was not evident to Isaac and Rebekah?

I certainly do not intend to rewrite scripture or act as a heretic by suggesting something we do not find within the Biblical text; but may I suggest that Jacob may have been misrepresented and falsely accused all these years? Of course he did plenty of things that were less than honorable, but I believe there was something within the fabric of Jacob's DNA that caused him to do and act the way that he did.

If Jacob was to be the recipient of the original blessing, birthright and inheritance, then why wasn't he born first? After all, it was only a matter of seconds before Jacob emerged after Esau, so close in fact that his hand was holding his brothers foot. I have given this great thought and would like to offer a suggestion as to what I believe took place before they were born.

In my opinion, Jacob, inside his mothers' womb, grabbed hold of something that was rightfully his to begin with. It wasn't a cognitive reaction but more of a spiritual response as he reached out and took a hold of his birthright. His innocence caused him to lash out and not let go of his promise from God. In other words, his spirit was grasping for the generational inheritance being passed down from his father and grandfather and his flesh acted accordingly, doing whatever he could to obtain that blessing.

Two nations were wrestling in Rebekah's womb. The fight within became very real and the internal struggles were evident as Jacob was in contention for his future in God. Did Esau actually steal Jacob's birthright and inheritance inside the womb by striving to be first born? Did the devil use Esau to rob Jacob of his God-given destiny? Jacob came out fighting, almost as if he was saying to Esau as he latched on to his heel, "Give me back what is rightfully mine! You stole that from me!" All the while, God was well aware of the birth order. He knew who would be born first, hence the Word spoken about the older serving the younger. But we are left wondering what truly transpired between the two brothers (nations) before they even entered into the world.

Another question remains to be asked: Why was Esau so willing to give up his birthright so easily?

"Behold, I am about to die; so of what use then is the birthright to me?" And Jacob said, "First swear to me"; so he swore to him, and sold his birthright to Jacob. Then Jacob gave Esau bread and lentil stew; and he ate and drank, and rose and went on his way. Thus Esau despised his birthright."
Gen. 25:32-34 (New American Standard Bible)

Esau despised his birthright; but why? And why was he so willing to give it up in exchange for a bowl of soup? Clearly, he had no regard for his inheritance and thus handled it irresponsibly. Jacob, on the other hand, just happened to be waiting for the opportune time to regain that which he believed was rightfully his.

Esau's disdain for his birthright lends even more evidence to the notion that he may have known it wasn't truly his to begin with. Why else would he have given up his position as the first-born child so easily? Maybe he knew that he had unrightfully passed Jacob in the womb and exited ahead of his brother. Genesis 25:22(NKJV) tells us that, *"the children struggled together within her."* No matter how we look at the scripture, one thing is for sure: Esau rejected his birthright.

One last observation about Jacobs birth.

When her days to be delivered were fulfilled, behold, there were twins in her womb. Now the first came forth red, all over like a hairy garment; and they named him Esau. Afterward his brother came forth with his hand holding on to Esau's heel, so his name was called Jacob; and Isaac was sixty years old when she gave birth to them. Gen. 25:24-26 (NASB)

The underlined verse clearly defines that Isaac and Rebekah named their children. God saw Jacob as Israel, not by the name his parents called him at birth. What am I getting at? Well I'm glad you asked.

Isaac and Rebekah named Jacob, a 'heal grabber' or as he is commonly known, a Supplanter; 'one who takes the place of another through force or scheming.' (dictionary.com). What if they misinterpreted what they saw, and instead of seeing a Supplanter they should have seen a Visionary? Or maybe if they had correctly interpreted the season of discomfort Rebekah was going through and paid attention to the word of the Lord they would have had a different perspective of the events leading up to and during the birth.

"Two nations are in your womb,
and two peoples from within you will be separated;
one people will be stronger than the other,
and the older will serve the younger." Gen. 25:21-23 (NIV)

Throughout most of Jacob's life every time his name was called, every time he was spoken too, every conversation that involved him, the name 'Supplanter' was constantly being spoken over his life. You and I both understand very clearly that if you proclaim something over yourself or someone else long enough they take on the nature and character of that proclamation. It begins to define a person, whether good or bad. So its no wonder Jacob acted the way he did. Right?

I don't need to belabor this point any longer, I think you get the gist of what I'm saying.

I realize this challenges traditional thinking regarding these passages of scripture and how it applies to our own lives. But let's be honest for a moment, who really understands the whole picture of the circumstances and unfolding events in your life except God? There are simply some things that God does not allow us to see until He reveals them at certain points as we progress along this journey. I guess that's why we walk by faith and not by sight and that's just the way God likes to operate.

As in Jacobs case I'm certainly not suggesting that we manipulate and deceive others to get what is rightfully ours; that would get us into some serious trouble with God. I am however attempting to illuminate our ability to assume certain things by what we see in the natural and clothe them with our own understanding, when in fact the complete opposite may be taking place.

Jacob was far from perfect, but he did have a specific purpose in the grand scheme of Gods greater plan. He was God's intended; the man of the hour through whom God would continue his generational blessing. God's responsibility was to prepare and orchestrate seasons and situations that would guide Jacob along a designed pathway. It was Jacobs's responsibility to embrace the change and receive the promise.

"There is a destiny for all of us, but unless we grasp a hold of its heels, we will never fully appreciate what God has called us to do." Paul Barratt

Every person is born with a purpose. We have seen great men and women throughout history achieve levels of greatness: Steve Jobs, Henry Ford, Mother Theresa, Martin Luther King, Jr. Abraham Lincoln, and countless more who had a specific purpose and destiny to fulfill. All had seasons in their lives were they had to change so they could embrace a future that was seeking to be made manifest. The reality of events they were faced with presented them with a choice, a choice to change or remain as they were. They embraced the change. Jacob embraced the change.

YOU ARE JUST LIKE YOUR FATHER!

Jacob was good at holding on (both literally and figuratively) until he accomplished his own goals. His ability to use a situation to benefit himself was not something he had conceived alone. His father, Isaac, and his grandfather, Abraham, also twisted the truth on occasion. This appears to be a family trait that followed this family from one generation to the next. Sound familiar? Have you ever had someone tell you that you are "just like your father?" There is a spiritual dynamic that affects all of our lives and can pass from one generation to the next. It's a seed that puts a chink in our armor and thrives and functions every day, sometimes undetected, unless we allow the Holy Spirit to identify it and choose to have it removed from our lives.

I have told my kids, "I don't want you to be just like me or your mother. I want you to be who Christ made you to be." I don't want them to embrace my faults and say kind words to puff me up as a parent. Even though I appreciate their kind words, love, and respect, but I'm no hero. God has certainly performed many surgeries on my life to get me where I am right now. All I ask of anyone, especially my children, is to "follow me as I follow Christ."

The beginning stages of our lives are out of our control. From early childhood we begin to exhibit certain characteristics and traits that are evident in our families. We act out what we see, hear, and feel in the environment in which we are raised. Think about it; how do we develop likes and dislikes? We form our personal worldviews by the information we are exposed to in our homes, environments, and cultures.

Jacob was raised in a Jewish Hebraic culture where certain established principles of living were adhered to and his mother was a major influence in his life. Scripture even tells us that Isaac loved Esau and Rebekah loved Jacob (Gen. 25:28 NAS). She most certainly trained him with the ability to get whatever he wanted. She was an integral part of his upbringing; therefore, what he witnessed and heard from her he trusted to be right and true. The same can be said for most of us – that we are products of the environment from which we came. We are all raised with a cultural mindset of how we should operate; how we walk, talk, work, our prejudices, political opinions, lifestyles and so on. I am not talking about a color or ethnicity, but an established mindset of principles and actions. However, once we come to the saving knowledge of the Lord Jesus Christ, His Kingdom culture should take priority in our lives. I was raised a specific way and I am proud of my heritage, but I know that I must submit my natural, cultural upbringing to the culture of the Kingdom I am now a part of.

GENERATIONS OF CHANGE

As each generation emerges, they are given a spiritual DNA that is unique to them. God operates in seasons, or "epochs" of time. He is the same yesterday, today and forever; he is still God, his son died upon the cross, Jesus is Lord, the blind see, the deaf hear, the dead are raised and salvation is free. But to each generation He appears in a different way. Just listen to music today as compared to 10 or 15 years ago; times change and so do we. This young generation has a uniqueness that has been deposited into them by the Spirit of God.

I would like to call it the change model—the constant advancement and forward motion of life caused by an evolution of ideas, concepts and innovations. It's like the old saying goes, "Change is here to stay!" The generations following us will serve the same God as you and I, but they will look, smell, and sound different than us. Will we allow them to fully express themselves in God, or will our hands control and manipulate them for our own agenda? It's up to us to allow them to be all that God has called them to be, regardless of how different it looks.

Jacob was different and unconventional in his approach to obtaining his future. He had to figure out where he fit in. The way he went about obtaining a birthright and inheritance was to some illegal and perceived as manipulative, but once he connected with his true identity and recognized what he was holding inside he became equipped to be a world-changer for the glory of God.

Most of us are familiar with Romans 8:28 (NKJV): "All things work together for good to them that love God, to them who are the called according to His purpose." Yet the very circumstances we find ourselves in at times feel like they're destroying us. Sometimes you may want to get off the ride, but for what? Sometimes you may find yourself faced with people who do not understand you or may even dislike you and it's hard to figure out why; but God always has a plan. Maybe you feel stuck in the middle of an impossible situation and the chariots of Pharaoh are chasing you down and the waves of the Red Sea are lapping at your feet. Let trust and faith in God arise. He will take the wheels off your enemy's chariots and part the Red Sea as you walk across on dry ground. In other words, trust in Him no matter the situation. Even when it seems as though your birthright has been stolen from you, even when nothing makes sense anymore, God always makes a way. He will always bring you back into your destiny even if it appears as though you have lost your way.

The uncomfortable place of the unknown creates the foundation for God to perform the miraculous as He manipulates our environment for his perfect purpose. If we accept his call, we will be changed forever. If we don't, it will haunt us for the rest of our days. There is a destiny for you to take hold of. Grasp the heel of what God has promised you as his servant and friend.

For those who may know what God has called you to do, be patient. It can only come to pass in His timing, and it will if you allow Him to work in your life. For those of you that don't know your purpose, I encourage you to seek the Lord and ask Him to reveal His dream for your life and destiny. But whether you know your calling, think you know, or are waiting for it to be revealed to you, know that He is God and holds your life in the palm of his hands. Hold on to what God has promised, grasp it with every fiber of your being and get ready for the ride of your life.

CHAPTER 3

THE ENCOUNTER

Although we are not told that Rebekah was present when Jacob acquired Esau's birthright, we are forced to question whether or not she was at least watching the saga of her two sons unfold. Maybe Jacob did do the right thing and told his mother what he had done. It doesn't really say. Why am I suggesting this? When Rebekah overheard Isaac talking to Esau about his pending departure she approached Jacob with the idea of inheriting the blessing that was to be bestowed upon the first-born. She must have been inspired by some past event to warrant such manipulative tendencies. Jacob went along with the idea even though he was hesitant at first.

"Jacob answered his mother, "Behold, Esau my brother is a hairy man and I am a smooth man. "Perhaps my father will feel me, then I will be as a deceiver in his sight, and I will bring upon myself a curse and not a blessing." But his mother said to him, "Your curse be on me, my son; only obey my voice, and go, get them for me." Gen. 27:11-13 (NASB)

We have read the account of how Jacob disguised himself as his brother, knowing that his father was too blind to see that he wasn't Esau and then receive the blessing (Genesis 27 (NASB). But once again we find Jacob in a questionable position. As I noted in Chapter 2, was this again another opportunity to fully obtain what was rightfully his to begin with? And due to his old nature, was this the only way he knew how to operate when under the influence and direction of his mother?

This was the last straw for Esau. He had lost the birthright and now the blessing. The atmosphere was filled with regret, disappointment and hatred. Esau was out for blood and Rebekah heard about it.

Jacob fled at the request of his mother, but she first had to have him released by his father. Once again, we find Rebekah twisting the situation to benefit her and her son. She skillfully spoke with Isaac, explaining to him that her life would basically be over if Jacob were to take a wife from the daughters of Heth (Genesis 27:46 (NAS), Isaac immediately called Jacob and sent him on his way to see Laban, Rebekah's brother.

"So Isaac called Jacob and blessed him and charged him, and said to him, "You shall not take a wife from the daughters of Canaan. Arise, go to Paddan-aram, to the house of Bethuel your mother's father; and from there take to yourself a wife from the daughters of Laban your mother's brother."
Gen. 28:1-2 (NASB)

Jacob was running scared, but unbeknownst to him, he was running directly into an appointment with God. Two worlds were on a collision course, a divine intersection of life, that God had ordained and purposed while Jacob was totally oblivious to his heavenly Father working in the background.

The uniqueness of God is that He simply uses situations and circumstances to direct our paths in ways that appear very uncomfortable, yet are intentionally designed to move us from one place to the next. Jacob knew where he was going geographically, but wasn't prepared for what awaited him along the way. As Jacob journeyed to see Laban and escape the clutches of his brother, he came upon a place to rest for the night where he witnessed a vision from heaven:

Now Jacob went out from Beersheba and went toward Haran. So he came to a certain place and stayed there all night, because the sun had set. And he took one of the stones of that place and put it at his head, and he lay down in that place to sleep. Then he dreamed, and behold, a ladder was set up on the earth, and its top reached to heaven; and there the angels of God were ascending and descending on it. And behold, the Lord stood above it and said:

"I am the Lord God of Abraham your father and the God of Isaac; the land on which you lie I will give to you and your descendants. Also your descendants shall be as the dust of the earth; you shall spread abroad to the west and the east, to the north and the south; and in you and in your seed all the families of the earth shall be blessed. Behold, I am with you and will keep you wherever you go, and will bring you back to this land; for I will not leave you until I have done what I have spoken to you." Then Jacob awoke from his sleep and said, "Surely the Lord is in this place, and I did not know it."
Gen. 28:10-16 (NKJV)

Divine encounters with God can happen when we least expect them and in Jacob's case he was completely caught off guard when the Lord appeared. Only God can bring about the perfect scenario to get our attention - for Jacob it was exhaustion, passed out on a rock and running for his life.

An incredible vision with incredible promises under an open heaven was given to Jacob; there was no mistaking the hand of God in what Jacob witnessed. What more could he ask for? What better time to receive a word than when he was truly between "a rock and a hard place?" Jacob needed an intervention and he received just that.

"For the vision is yet for an appointed time,
but at the end it shall speak, and not lie:

though it tarry, wait for it;
because it will surely come, it will not tarry. "
Habakkuk 2:3 (NKJV)

YOU CAN RUN BUT YOU CAN'T HIDE

When our attention is focused on self-preservation, we can easily miss the road signs along life's highway. God creates opportunities at strategic junctures in our lives, usually between a closed door behind us and an open door before us in the form of a divine encounter. It is an amazing transformation to watch God take an overwhelming problem and turn it into a glorious event. What makes it even more incredible is that God always finds a way to get the glory, especially when we find ourselves saying, "I can't believe God just did that!"

Jacobs' years as a child were undoubtedly filled with listening to stories from his mother and father about their own journey, as well as that of his grandfather Abraham also. Their incredible lives of miracles, provision and encounters with Almighty God must have made for amazing bedtime stories. Like many believers, Jacob had heard of what God had done in the lives of others, but never had a true encounter for himself. Jacob knew about the power of God, yet had never truly experienced it for himself. Little did he know, his life was about to change.

Jacob found himself at a crossroads, exhausted from running and desperate for peace. His mind was surely replaying the events that had led to his hasty departure and was probably wondering how all of this mess had started - a bowl of soup, a fake disguise and a deceptive word. His life was spinning out of control, but Jacob was on a collision course with destiny. Jacob fell asleep; I honestly believe that he passed out due to complete exhaustion and then a deep sleep came upon him.

There have been times in my life where the only way God could get my undivided attention was to speak as I was sleeping; a place where I was void of all outside influences, circumstances and distractions and He would speak in the form of a dream or vision. God can speak whenever and however He desires to, especially when His word doesn't get interrupted with the business of our day and the interruptions of darkness. A Holy Ghost anesthesia came upon Jacob and God revealed Himself.

We can only imagine the flood of emotions running through Jacob's mind and spirit as he awoke. This had never happened to him before – something so incredible, so profound, it could only be God. There was no other explanation. Overcome by this monumental event, Jacob erected a memorial in that place – a place he would never forget for the rest of his life.

When you receive a dream from the Lord, and it has to be from Him, the dream establishes a marker or position in your present day that speaks of your future, a place where God gives you a glimpse of where He sees you. This may or may not be your final destiny, but it speaks of a destination you are navigating towards. It is of vital importance that you write the event down exactly as God revealed it. You will need it as a reference point for your next season.

There are times in our lives when we really need an encounter with God - a word, a dream, a vision, something that tells us we are on the right track. As we look to Him in the midst of our circumstances, our desperation cultivates an atmosphere for the miraculous move of God in our lives and I guarantee that He will speak to you.

God has appeared in my life on many occasions and it has often been at times where I had reached a crossroads and was faced with a decision. The pressure was on and if I made the wrong choice it had the ability to set me back months, maybe even years. My wife and I needed a word from God, we were desperate, and even though at times we felt like we were taking our last breath, He never disappointed us.

As we met with God in different seasons and upon life's highway, it was so important to make a memorial of the personal encounters we had with Him. This not only testifies of the goodness of God, but it allowed us to see the incredible journey we had been on.

IT HAD TO BE YOU

Whenever God brings about an adjustment in our lives He is consistent about bringing uncontested confirmation. He brings us to a place of understanding where we know there is no other explanation than, "it had to be God!"

Jacob's encounter was so significant that in Genesis 28:16 (NASB) he tells us, *"Surely the Lord is in this place and I did not know it."* He who reigns always has a way of getting our attention, even in the most unconventional ways. He wants to show his glory to his believers and God simply performs the miraculous to warrant our undivided attention. If He can get Moses' attention with a burning bush and Jacob's attention with a ladder from heaven, then He will use all at his disposal to get yours.

Following God's appearance to Jacob in the midst of his crisis, his outlook changed from a man on the run to an individual with a purpose. The landscape changed in the eyes of Jacob and he began to see things differently. Suddenly, there was color where there had been gloom and doom, suddenly there was purpose for his living.

Change your current situation by the Word of the Lord and begin to paint a portrait of the way God sees you in the future.

Jacob needed a new perspective on things. If he had gone in to Laban's camp before having this encounter with God, then he probably would have missed his destiny because of a clouded vision and a broken focus. God created an opportunity for Jacob and it was his choice whether or not to embrace it. He had seen firsthand God's plan and purpose for his life and it was up to him to move into that which was revealed.

It is necessary to know that as we move forward into our individual and corporate destinies that God does indeed provide distinct road signs along the way. Without them we would stray from the path He has set before us. Whether it is in a dream, a vision, or a prophetic word, God will speak and He will have the last word. However, it bears repeating that it is ultimately our choice.

CHAPTER 4

JACOB'S DESTINY

After a night he would never forget, Jacob continued his journey toward Haran where he came upon some shepherds waiting to water their flocks. Unsure of who they were, he inquired of them. Then, Rachel suddenly appeared before him. It was said of Jacob that he lifted his voice and wept (Genesis. 29:11 (NLT). Exhilaration ensued as his heart connected with something and someone he had been looking for all his life.

"While he (Jacob) was still talking with them, Rachel came with her father's sheep, for she was a shepherd. When Jacob saw Rachel daughter of his uncle Laban, and Laban's sheep, he went over and rolled the stone away from the mouth of the well and watered his uncle's sheep. Then Jacob kissed Rachel and began to weep aloud. He had told Rachel that he was a relative of her father and a son of Rebekah. So she ran and told her father. As soon as Laban heard the news about Jacob, his sister's son, he hurried to meet him. He embraced him and kissed him and brought him to his home, and there Jacob told him all these things." Gen. 29:9-13 (NIV)

DIVINE ALIGNMENT

Call it what you will – a chance meeting, being at the right place at the right time, even serendipity - Jacob entered into a season that had been orchestrated by the hand of God in the form of a divine encounter with destiny.

There is something powerful that takes place when every area of your life begins to converge into a beautifully choreographed dance or a musical symphony. No one can put the pieces together like God. He connects our past to our present and to our future, building a collage of seasons and experiences that, at the right time and at the right place, unveils the very purpose for which we were born.

Deep within all of us is a cry to be used by God in a specific way. And within that cry of our heart is a passion and a dream that speaks of a future that can be seen but has not yet manifested. This dream could be something you connected with as a young child or something that captivated your attention as an adult - a vision, an inspiration - something that was unique to only you and you saw yourself doing it.

Some of us have received prophetic words over our lives that spoke about the future, some have received engaging dreams that resonated with our heart and within our spirit. All of them powerful, all of them exciting. But how do you get there? How do all the pieces of the puzzle come together? Jacob was no different.

God had given him the end game narrative in Gen. 28:10-16, the dream where Jacob saw angels ascending and descending from heaven and God speaking a powerful Word. How would Jacob do this? God had to put something, or in this case someone, in his life that captivated his heart to fulfill the generational call of God on his life.

There is a favorite scripture of mine that goes like this;

So will My word be which goes forth from My mouth;
It will not return to Me empty,
Without accomplishing what I desire,
And without succeeding in the matter for which I sent it.
Isaiah 55:11 (NASB)

Gods desire is for His word to continue on from one generation to the next, promoting and advancing the Kingdom of God in and through His people. The end game (if I can call it that) is to accomplish the fulfillment of His word and the Kingdom of God throughout all mankind. And He placed you here to be a part of that plan. We may only see part of that plan for ourselves and our family but God sees it hundreds of years down the road. We are an intricate network of believers, all connected with one common goal in mind. The Kingdom of God. We are all a very important piece in the grand scheme of the plan of God.

What is your part? It is the combining of your Gifts, Talents and Abilities, your life experiences, coupled with the dream, passion or desire God has put in your heart, that reaches a point where they all come together and you find yourself doing the very thing God called you to do.

I know this sounds repetitive, as I had alluded to this earlier, but we need to know that there is far more to our circumstances than we could ever understand.

Jacobs destiny was Rachel. This was Gods plan for him to fulfill the word over his life and continue on with the generational impact. But that word came with a lot of responsibilities and requirements, as we will discuss later.

Now with all that being said, there are certain things that present themselves in your life that can, if not corrected, rob you of that dream.

35

DREAM STEALERS

God has equipped all of us with a particular grouping of gifts and talents that are tailor made for the specific role we are called to in life for the Kingdom of God. This could include anything, from becoming a successful business owner in a major city or a 2nd grade teacher in an impoverished community, an elected official in an affluent city or a police office in the worst part of town. But because of what life throws at us, and the uncertainty of choices we make, we often lose sight of those dreams and passions. We set them aside for other people and other things in our lives. We start a family, a new career, we relocate geographically which are all great things, please don't get me wrong, but its the wrong choices and setbacks we make along the way that tend to separate us more and more from our future. The further you separate yourself from the call of God the harder it is to make that journey back. But please be encouraged! Your destiny and purpose never disappeared, and it is still available. All that God has for you is still there, waiting for you to re-engage your passion in the right season of your life. We really do serve a patient God.

This is very important for us to grasp because a lot of people that became side-tracked over the years, for one reason or another, have come to the conclusion that because they gave up on their call that it's no longer available to them. That's not necessarily the case. God's word will not return to Him void. Remember? So the word is still alive and active. Reconnecting with that word may seem like a long road back but God has the ability to accelerate time on your behalf.

I truly believe the DNA that God has placed within all of us pulls us toward our future, it acts like a magnetic force drawing us into the unknown. Our life's journey is not only to navigate us back into the arms of Almighty God, but also to the purpose for which we were divinely designed.

God is supreme and sovereign in all that He does. It may be one glimpse into the mysteries and secrets of God that provides us with the passion to persevere. But what if that momentary glimpse takes 5, 10 or even 30 years to materialize? What then? Can you make it? Do you truly trust God?

Is it easy? Absolutely not. Is it worth the wait? Yes.

YOU DON'T HAVE TO BE ALONE

Part of our journey involves meeting other people. These crucial individuals whom God divinely brings into our lives are potential keys to our "next level" in life. I call them divine appointments.

Jacob had his first divine appointment with God, then Laban, then Leah and finally with Rachel. They all played a significant role in his advancement toward his destiny. The key is having the discernment to identify these appointments as being from God.

It benefits us most when we pray for God to send the right people into our sphere of influence. We cannot go it alone and we do not have all the know-how to get to where we are going. We need quality individuals and leaders in our lives to help guide, direct, and equip us.

Without others cheering us on we would retreat into a corner, depressed and self-centered. The battle between the flesh and the spirit is not to be fought alone; we need others to lift up our arms when the weight gets too heavy and the battle to fierce. Watch for those who have battle scars, who have stood the test of time and come through the fire and the flood, those who are mature in the faith and have witnessed God do the miraculous. These are the generals you want to sit under and learn from, not the rookie who has been nowhere and done nothing but has all the answers.

Let God grow you by allowing him to stretch you. God can place certain people in your life just to tick-you-off; how are you approaching that? Are you calling down fire and brimstone or is there a heart of compassion reaching out to that person? There may be another individual, a leader, who has required you to do certain things that you feel are beneath you. Ask yourself "what needs to change in me first?" Then, be open to see what God works in and out of your life. Obtain the right perspective; don't use others to advance your agenda and climb the spiritual corporate ladder, but instead see the Hand of God operating in your life and in the lives of others around you.

Let us never get stuck at home plate by failing to follow the simple foundational principles of Godly living: loving God, serving, giving, treating others as you want to be treated, living in peace, reading His word, and prayer. If we don't follow the simple things, then how can we expect Him to give us more?

IT'S WORTH THE WAIT

Jacob knew what he wanted (Rachel) and was prepared to stay in one location and wait seven years for his lovely bride. The one mistake he made was putting a time limit on the event. Don't restrict God to your timing. He's not obligated to give you a set time and date so we must genuinely trust and wait on Him.

Laban was obliging enough to accept the time frame set by Jacob, but he had another plan. We can set time lines for obtaining certain goals in our lives, which isn't a bad thing, but once we begin doing the same with God, we find ourselves disappointed when it doesn't work out the way we had planned.

Then Laban said to Jacob, "Because you are my relative, should you therefore serve me for nothing? Tell me, what should your wages be?" Now Laban had two daughters: the name of the elder was Leah, and the name of the younger was Rachel. Leah's eyes were delicate, but Rachel was beautiful of form and appearance. Now Jacob loved Rachel; so he said, "I will serve you seven years for Rachel your younger daughter." And Laban said, "It is better that I give her to you than that I should give her to another man. Stay with me." So Jacob served seven years for Rachel, and they seemed only a few days to him because of the love he had for her. Gen. 29:15-20 (NKJV)

We have all heard the phrase "time flies when you're having fun" and in Jacob's case it was as if time had accelerated for him. As Jacob came to the end of his seven years, he positioned himself to receive his destiny, only to find that the one thing he had waited for all his life was still beyond his grasp.

The most disappointing of occasions in the life of a believer is the anticipation of a season where you know - according to the signs along the highway, the words, the people and the situations – that it has to be your turn and your season is upon you. You think, "I have arrived!" Only to find that time passed beyond the calendar that you had set for this appointment with destiny. A majority of people quit at this point only to believe that it was too good to be true and that they must have made a mistake. Some even make the statement; "I missed it. What did I do wrong?" Frustration and disappointment rapidly emerge and the proverbial beating of the head against the wall ensues.

But hold on! Remember the memorial that you erected when you encountered God for the first time? Fear not, for it fans the flames again of the passion that resides within you, propelling you forward in the midst of total let-down, giving you hope that keeps your heart expectant for the greater good. God does not lie and He will not fail you. We fail ourselves by telling Him when and where we expect our lives to happen.

There are many times in my life where I put time constraints upon God only to awake the next day to find life as normal with no dramatic event that had taken place. In fact, I have awakened to multiple problems that had unbelievably compiled overnight. How did this happen when I was so sure this time, things would be different? Yet disappointment came knocking one more time. Not unlike Jacob.

WELCOME TO YOUR LEAH SEASON.

CHAPTER 5

THE LEAH SEASON

He'd made it. Seven years and no sign of Esau, Jacob thought he was safe and sound. He had an awesome wife-to-be, an amazing father-in-law, and life was good...except for one minor detail:

Then Jacob said to Laban, "Give me my wife. My time is completed, and I want to make love to her." So Laban brought together all the people of the place and gave a feast. But when evening came, he took his daughter Leah and brought her to Jacob, and Jacob made love to her. And Laban gave his servant Zilpah to his daughter as her attendant. When morning came, there was Leah! So Jacob said to Laban, "What is this you have done to me? I served you for Rachel, didn't I? Why have you deceived me?" Laban replied, "It is not our custom here to give the younger daughter in marriage before the older one. Gen. 29:21-26 (NIV)

Paraphrasing how Jacob must have really felt;

Shaken and profoundly stirred, Jacob emerged from his tent completely confused by the previous evening's events. His old nature erupted within him and Laban became the manipulator. In Jacob's eyes, he had ben deceived and Laban's actions were inconceivable, treacherous, and downright inexcusable. When the tables are turned,

41

life takes on a whole new perspective - Jacob had the wool pulled over his eyes and he didn't see this deception coming.

Just twenty-four hours before Laban revealed his cunning trickery, Jacob thought he had it all figured out. He believed he beat the odds and that his destiny awaited him in all its glory - Rachel. The promises of God were coming to pass and he could see Rachel bearing many children, his seed creating a nation. He was prepared to take his wife and his whole life was about to be complete. The word God had spoken to him was playing over and over in his mind. After all, he was running for his life and this word couldn't have come at a more crucial time:

"Your descendants will also be like the dust of the earth, and you will spread out to the west and to the east and to the north and to the south; and in you and in your descendants shall all the families of the earth be blessed." Gen. 28:14 (NASB)

Laban was operating in the established law of culture in his family and there was nothing Jacob could do about it. As he longed for Rachel, he was suddenly faced with Leah.

EMBRACING YOUR LEAH SEASON

There is a Leah Season for every believer who chooses to be used of God. It often comes without warning, but expect it to disrupt your plans as you begin to look around and declare "LIFE MAKES NO SENSE!"

I could have chosen any man or woman of God in the Bible as a platform to write this book - Abraham's ram in the thicket, Joseph's dream, Moses and the burning bush, David and the cave at Adullam, Elijah and the Brook of Cherith - examples of those who met with God during a specific season in their life. That season brought about life changing events. The examples are endless, but each one illustrates a common thread of significant transformation and a changing landscape in their life. The Leah Season proves to be an exhilarating and, at times, challenging journey but its rewards are everlasting. These seasons can be difficult in nature and the behind-the-scenes dealings of God can leave us with many unanswered questions, but they ultimately launch us into our glorious destiny.

I believe there is a little bit of Jacob in all of us, which is why we find him so relatable. Jacob quickly realized that he was no longer in control, and what took place shook him to his core. Like jumping out of an airplane and finding out you forgot to pack your parachute, Jacob's idea of what things were supposed to look like turned out to be quite the opposite. He did question Laban but to no avail. In the end, Jacob was in Laban's territory and he was the boss.

Jacob was accustomed to getting his own way. Even when he passionately pursued Rachel, he knew that the younger daughter would not be given before the first born. However, to Jacob, that was nothing more than an obstacle to overcome, and he believed that he would. Why do you think he initiated the barter system with Laban and promised to work for his daughter for seven years? He was playing on Laban's emotions and attempting to manipulate the situation. Laban, of course, was not that gullible.

Why is it that we think we can jump ahead of the line, forgo the inevitable tests and trials and be elevated to a higher position when we don't have the experience or capacity to receive what God has for us? As new generations appear on the horizon and new technologies, concepts, and ideas emerge and the pace of life gathers more and more speed. As believers, we fall into that same pace of life - faster, faster, faster. This inevitably creates a lack of patience and rather than wait on God, we end up getting off track. In our minds, He is not moving fast enough so we interject our own agendas and do it our own way. The unfulfilled appetites of wants and needs intermingle to the point that nobody knows what they really want out of life or who they truly are anymore.

Here's what we need to know: The waiting produces character. The testing produces integrity. The anointing produces authority. And true patience will give you entry to your promised land. There is a right of passage that is earned through life's experiences by allowing God to build capacity in us. The key is for us to recognize what God is doing and benefit from the growth that takes place within us.

Jacob lived his life, from how others would have perceived it, by manipulating the situations and people around him. To him, it seemed as though he always got the raw end of the deal, so why not make the most out of every situation? His mind undoubtedly raced as he tried to make sense of all that had happened to him. The flood of emotions must have sent his head spinning; anger, bitterness, sorrow, resentment, disbelief, failure, loneliness, abandonment, disappointment. All overcame him as he tried to figure it out why his plan failed.

When contradictions and contentions come, and they will, we must recall the Word of the Lord over our lives. It will bring a peace and an anchor to the storms that are raging within. Resist the urge to spin out of control and speak against what God is doing. When events don't turn out the way you expect, it does not give you the right to be mad at God but it does give you the ability to discern what is taking place. Jacob declared in Genesis 28:16 *"Surely the Lord is in this place, and I did not know it."* (NASB) God is with you in the high places and the low. Rest in Him and praise Him through the storm. Know that He is in control and thank Him that you are not!

WATCH YOUR STEP

As I mentioned in the beginning of this book, we must rightly discern what comes from the devil and what comes from God. You may think that is easy to do, but I caution you to remember that your adversary is a sly opponent. What may look like a "right" door could very well be a trap set before you. On the contrary, what may appear as an uncomfortable place (the loss of a job, a geographical change, not getting that promotion) may also be the hand of God navigating you through a season toward fulfilling a specific role. Just because something looks different than the way you had imagined, don't immediately dismiss it as "not from God."

In Jacob's case, there was a reason for Leah to be a part of his life – a major part. But he did not understand that when she first arrived. In fact, Jacob never really paid much attention to Leah. He remembered what she looked like and was less than impressed. He was blinded by Rachel's beauty.

"There was no sparkle in Leah's eyes, but Rachel had a beautiful figure and a lovely face." Genesis 29:17 (NLT)

Jacob was not prepared for what happened after the honeymoon...and when the honeymoon is over, it's over! He had to wait again for his true bride. WAIT! A word we all love to hear.

Imagine, if you will for a moment, waking up every morning for seven years and seeing your destiny right before you, just beyond your reach. Rachel walked by Jacob's tent every day. His heart longed to be with her. He was captivated by her beauty, by the way she would walk and talk, the distinct fragrance from her hair and her clothes that would fill the atmosphere with her very presence. And with his heart aching, he would try to sleep at night, but could never get her out of his mind. He didn't have to see Rachel to know that she was close by; he could sense when his destiny was present. He had waited seven years for his bride and when it was time, he woke up with the wrong woman. OUCH!

WHAT ON EARTH HAPPENED?

I would dare say that part of the internal struggles we face and the pressures of life we experience on a daily basis are the very process God designed to equip us for the future. The added difficulties also come when the competing assignments of hell attempt to pull us from the path God has chosen for us. These events can often create great upheaval in our lives when we look at our future and see that it is way beyond our ability to reach it.

We can behold the manifested portion of what God has allowed us to preview; the vision, the dream and God's Word, but for a season we are not permitted to hold the fullness of it in our hands. Why then does God show us our future? He shows us so we can begin to faithfully move towards it, grow in capacity, be renewed in our mind and navigate through the seasons of change that prepare us for what lies ahead.

The Lord knows it takes time to bring us into our full potential, but more than that, He wants to know if we can be completely trusted with what He desires to release through us. If you can correctly steward the increase and influence He has placed in you by successfully passing through the different seasons of tests and trials, God will give you your mountain of inheritance. But realize that your inheritance will not come without a fight. The increase of provision, recognition and notoriety come with a price. All this and much more has the ability to make you a true ambassador in the Kingdom of God or a Judas in the court of the King.

What God is looking for is long-term effectiveness and investment. Slow intentional growth is growth that will last. In the hands of the right person, God will continue his purpose and destiny from generation to generation. If He can trust you with a little, He can trust you with greatness. Something's to consider as you move from season to season; how to faithfully conduct yourself before people, how to administrate His gifts, and how you live for God when no one else is watching. The epitome of integrity.

WHEN ALL SEEMS LOST

When God takes you to the backside of the desert, away from life itself, where the distance grows further and further from the reality of your dreams, where no one recognizes you anymore and the easy things of life become so difficult, look no further – this is Your Leah Season. The development of your gifts, talents, and character are honed when you don't have an audience and nobody knows your name. You're alone with God. What do you do then?

For seven years, my family and I relocated from Upstate New York to the mountains of Colorado. We went from a city of 200,000 people, 100 feet above sea level to a remote town of 3,000 people, 8,200 feet above sea level. It was one of the most picturesque places I have ever lived, but also one of the harshest climates, both naturally and spiritually. This was our wilderness journey, literally in the middle of nowhere. We met with God, we cried with God and we rejoiced with God. But it all served its purpose. Would I do it again? No. Would I have exchanged it for something else? No. The capacity that was built in us was the fulfillment of a prophetic word we had received years prior during which God said He would "take seven years of learning and condense it into three." Think about that for one second: does intense pressure come to mind?

How do you make it through such a season? By trusting and relying on God as though your life depended on it. In actuality, your life does depend on it! Without the stretching, pulling and growing in God, you will never be able to fully embrace and function in your destiny. When nothing makes sense, get hungry for God. The passionate pursuit of His presence will pull you in to incredible encounters with Him that cause your circumstances to pale in comparison. They may still be there in the morning, but they don't hold the high ground anymore when you spend time with Him.

WATCH WHAT YOU SAY

Jacob fulfilled his commitment to Laban and his marriage contract with Leah and stayed committed to what was required of him in that season. Even though he felt cornered, he completed the process. Without Leah, he would have aborted key people in the history of Israel. He was one man positioned in a local house but purposed to affect an entire nation.

You may have no idea who or what your Leah Season is or what her positioning represents in your life, but one thing is for sure – she is being prepared to enter your life for your benefit and divine advancement. It was impossible for Jacob to know to whom Leah would give birth. Not even Leah herself understood her complete destiny and purpose. But each birth represented specific seasons in her life and also held specific keys to Jacob's future.

God witnessed first-hand by Jacob's actions and comments that he hated the situation he was in and hated the fact that Leah was his wife. Don't think for a moment that our words have no effect on our future. God responded by opening Leah's womb and closing Rachel's.

"And he went in also unto Rachel, and he loved also Rachel more than Leah, and served with him yet seven other years. And when the LORD saw that Leah was hated, he opened her womb: but Rachel was barren." Gen. 29:30-31 (KJV)

How many times have we read the scriptures about Jacobs' life and skimmed over this passage, not realizing the power it reveals? If anything, it should speak volumes about the way we are dealing with our current situations. We hinder, curse, and delay the operation of God's word over our life when we speak against the author and finisher of our individual destinies and don't even realize we are doing it at the time. The devil does not have to work overtime wanting to rob, steal, and destroy from us when we do a pretty good job all by ourselves. The enemy of our soul just sits back and watches us sabotage our future with our own words.

Likewise, the tongue is a small part of the body, but it makes great boasts. Consider what a great forest is set on fire by a small spark. The tongue also is a fire, a world of evil among the parts of the body. It corrupts the whole body, sets the whole course of one's life on fire, and is itself set on fire by hell. James 3:5-6 (NIV)

If we can learn to understand and recognize the Leah Season in our lives, we will see how it impacts our todays and our tomorrows. This truly is where the rubber meets the road and our destiny hangs in the balance by the choices we make. Choices come in all shapes and sizes, but the one that holds the greatest influence is choosing to speak words that are positive, encouraging, and edifying over our lives.

I know what you may be thinking; "It's so hard to have a positive attitude when my whole life feels like it's falling apart!" Trust me; I understand how it feels. But believe me when I tell you that the very words that you speak will either keep you going around the proverbial mountain or give you the keys to enter your promised land. You may not always have the ability to control what takes place around you, but you certainly have the power to choose how you speak over your own life.

Some of you may be feeling a little discouraged right now because some of the decisions you have made were the wrong ones, but God truly is a forgiving God. When we turn to Him in repentance, ask for forgiveness and forgiving others, He moves mountains and dries up the riverbed so we can cross back over to the path He has designed for our lives. He will help you continue onward to destiny, but you must choose to follow and trust in Him.

God will give you your destiny as He gave Jacob his. You may have your eyes set on Rachel, but until Leah has served her purpose in your life, your destiny remains barren. Stay focused on the journey and lean not on your own understanding, but trust in Him always. Embrace your Leah so that you can one day fully enjoy your Rachel.

CHAPTER 6

LEAH AND RACHEL

Jacob was not going to let Rachel slip out of his hands over a technicality. He had labored for seven years to fulfill his commitment to Laban and one more week wasn't going to make that much of a difference. So the agreement was for Jacob to fulfill one week with Leah, after which he would receive Rachel's hand in marriage and agree to work an additional seven years of service for Laban. Many assume that Jacob had to wait a total of 14 years before he could take Rachel as his wife, but scripture clearly tells us otherwise:

And Laban said, "It must not be done so in our country, to give the younger before the firstborn. Fulfill her week, and we will give you this one also for the service which you will serve with me still another seven years." Then Jacob did so and fulfilled her week. So he gave him his daughter Rachel as wife also. And Laban gave his maid Bilhah to his daughter Rachel as a maid. Then Jacob also went in to Rachel, and he also loved Rachel more than Leah. And he served with Laban still another seven years. Gen 29:26-30 (NKJV)

Jacob seems to be faced with a major dilemma, or at least that's the way it appears at face value. However, within his current state of purpose, coupled with his future state of destiny, lies a methodical movement that would span history across many generations.

On one hand, Jacob appeared to be held captive by the events surrounding Leah and his contractual agreement with Laban. On the other hand, he longed to advance his destiny by marrying Rachel. Jacob was aware of his future and clearly knew what he wanted, but was forced to remain connected with his "present" purpose.

Creating a balance and an understanding of your 'present day' and your 'future to come' is vital, especially when both simultaneously intersect in your life. We achieve this balance by not being so future-bound that we actually disconnect from our present situation. We must also understand that we are not forever bound by our present circumstances and must embrace our future. In other words, that which appears to be far off will come closer as Leah accomplishes her purpose in your life. The past is done, today is here and tomorrow is but a few hours away. BALANCE.

Identify your priorities. Stay connected with God, remove distractions, envision yourself in the future, but embrace the present. Remain accountable to the voice of counsel and trust, trust, trust God. Then and only then will you reach your Rachel.

Although Laban may not win any awards for the best father-in-law in the world, he was a catalyst that produced a stable grounding for Jacob. When we consider that Jacob was to remain with Laban for fourteen years in accordance to his contract, seven years for Rachel and an additional seven more once he had married her, Jacob was in no position to run away when things got uncomfortable. He had too much to lose.

TIME TO GO?

Have you ever wanted to walk away from it all when the pressure becomes so overwhelming that you feel like you're going to literally explode? The yoke of God that fastens you to a certain place is designed to allow you the necessary components of growth, appointments, alignment, and timing. God will keep you stationary until the day of your release. Even when you want to escape, you can't because there's nowhere to go.

Remember the ones that God has brought into your life to be voices of wise counsel? This is where they become vitally important. You must have the right people, sent by God, to help you navigate through these times. I cannot emphasize this enough that these people must be trustworthy, credible, and mature in the Lord. Anyone else is not worth your time because one wrong word can have serious ramifications. You have to know that God sent you the right people. If you go it alone you will likely fail. The moment you deviate from the focus of your purpose and destiny (both present and future), and become side tracked to follow another path, you create a disconnect in your walk. As scripture teaches us in James 1:8;

"Such people should not expect to receive anything from the Lord. Their loyalty is divided between God and the world, and they are unstable in everything they do." (NLT)
This is a very dangerous place to be.

Over the last few chapters we have discussed your past, present and future – the combination of seasons you have experienced and the ones that are upon you. However, it is very important for you to understand that once you have destiny in hand, you cannot simply eliminate Leah. Jacob was not free to do as he pleased; he still had a contract to fulfill. You see, Leah and Rachel were not meant to be independent of each other; they were designed to work together. Leah kept Rachel in check and Rachel kept Leah in check. If all that Jacob saw was Rachel and his future, he would have turned his back on Leah and missed half of the blessing that awaited him.

Consequently, if all that Jacob saw was Leah and his present situation, he would have no hope for a future with Rachel.

Even though Rachael was his destiny, Leah and her children represented the seasons in Jacob's life that brought him to his divine appointment with destiny. You will always have the memories of how God brought you through each season, the incredible journey, the waiting period, the frustration of the daily grind, and the mountains to climb.

This entire spectrum of emotion expressed in one collage of experience ends with a new beginning. A place where you are totally alive, doing what you are called to do, living life to its fullest and having a great time doing it.

As I mentioned earlier, if you can see your future, you can possess it. It's the process of obtaining it that separates the fighter from the quitter. Your life was never designed to be easy, but it is designed to be monumental.

IT'S NOT OVER UNTIL IT'S OVER!

Laban required Jacob to fulfill a week with Leah and promised to then give him Rachel. But simply receiving your destiny is not enough; God also requires periods and seasons of further development, instruction and the walking out of the fullness of what He has entrusted you to do. Remember the same people that you looked to for guidance in the tough times? These same people will help keep you grounded and accountable in times of abundance.

Character, integrity, and accountability must always remain high on your list of values as you walk out your destiny. More importantly, stay close to God. Your relationship with Him brought you through the Leah Season and that same relationship will take you into the fullness for which you were created. It only takes a momentary lapse of judgment, an immoral slip, or a poor decision and suddenly the downhill momentum begins. Be wise.

Jacob found out the hard way that destiny didn't come the way he thought it would. Waiting one more week for Rachel didn't deter him but he still remained unaware of the fact that through his relationship with Leah they would give birth to the Levitical priesthood through Levi and the Messianic bloodline through Judah. We must take account of our actions in seasons such as these and not allow ourselves to miss what God is doing. As with so many of us our pit becomes our promotion and our frustration becomes our fulfillment but there is so much that gets fulfilled in the Leah Season that has an impact on generations to come that can easily be missed. For Jacob his destiny was already being fulfilled, he just couldn't see the whole picture.

THANK GOD FOR THE KIDS

Out of Jacob came the twelve tribes of Israel. Leah birthed six sons plus one daughter and her handmaid, Bilhah, birthed two boys. Rachel also gave birth to two sons and her handmaid Zilpah gave birth to two more boys. All of the children held their places in history as well as in Jacob's destiny, but let's just focus on Leah's children. You may be surprised at the direct correlation each have to the seasons in Jacob's life as well as what they represent for you.

REUBEN

"Leah conceived and bore a son and named him Reuben, for she said, 'Because the LORD has seen my affliction; surely now my husband will love me.'" Gen 29:32 (NASB)

Reuben represents a season where nothing adds up or even makes any sense. This beginning stage of the Leah Season brings to surface; frustration, misunderstandings, conflicts, and difficulties. God does not seem to be speaking and the affliction has stopped up your hearing, but the pressure is still being applied. People wonder what your problem is and the only ones who do understand are the ones that have gone through the process themselves.

SIMEON

"Then she conceived again and bore a son and said, 'Because the LORD has heard that I am unloved, He has therefore given me this son also.; So she named him Simeon."
Gen 29:33 (NASB)

This is the voice of desperation in a season where words begin to form on your lips as you cry out to God for the understanding of your plight. You're looking for answers to your life's purpose that He has ordained for you. The greatest cry that can come from any believer is the one that comes from their innermost being - deep calling unto deep, a cry only heard by God Himself. You are desperate to hear a word from God, and our heavenly Father responds to a desperate hunger from His child.

LEVI

"She conceived again and bore a son and said, 'Now this time my husband will become attached to me, because I have borne him three sons.' Therefore he was named Levi."
Gen.29:34 (NASB)

Levi represents a joining together of your voice with the heart of God, creating the divine attachment he has been waiting for. God never goes away in the midst of your crisis; he remains with you all the time. You may think he has hidden himself from you, but on the contrary, he has been interceding for you, calling you closer and calling you higher. This is an unmistakable sound of two worlds coming together, heaven and earth, forming a supernatural tsunami of purpose and destiny.

JUDAH

"And she conceived again and bore a son and said, 'This time I will praise the LORD.' Therefore she named him Judah. Then she stopped bearing." Gen 29:35 (NASB)

Judah represents the joyful response of praise and celebration as God shows up in the midst of your season, putting His finger on the pulse of your heart and positioning you toward destiny. The divine transitioning from discomfort to a place of praise and worship creates that portal of entry where you encounter and escape in to the presence of an Almighty and powerful God. A great peace descends upon you, the storms subside, the waves bow down as Jesus climbs into your boat.

ISSACHAR

"God gave heed to Leah, and she conceived and bore Jacob a fifth son. Then Leah said, 'God has given me my wages because I gave my maid to my husband.' So she named him Issachar". Gen. 30: 17 – 18 (NASB)

Issachar represents the reward for staying the course, the fulfillment within us declaring the bold statement that 'in Christ we made it through the fire and the flood.' There is something to be said of those that remain faithful to the cause of Christ. No matter what they endure, they stay true to the journey set before them. When you think you are down-for-the-count, God rewards those who diligently seek him.

ZEBULUN

"Leah conceived again and bore a sixth son to Jacob. Then Leah said, 'God has endowed me with a good gift; now my husband will dwell with me, because I have borne him six sons.' So she named him Zebulun." Gen 30:19-20 (NASB)

Zebulun represents a special place in God – a dwelling place with Him; a unique place of total surrender and complete peace, a promotion into his glory unmatched by any other event in your life. This is the secret place of his dwelling, abiding under the shadow of the Almighty. Here, nothing else matters but Him. When a believer reaches a position of total dependence upon God, He is able to trust us with much more because He first trusted us with little.

DINAH

"Afterward she bore a daughter and named her Dinah."
Gen 30:21 (NASB)

We all remember the names of the twelve males born and positioned as the Tribes of Israel, (six of which were just named) but a daughter that almost went unrecognized and forgotten bares a significant closure to the Leah Season. She was never mentioned as a Tribe and to some she may even have been considered a mistake. Dinah was her name and she represented justice.

Most times we equate the word justice as a response to an act of injustice but I submit to you a dictionary version of this word as it applies to all of us;

JUSTICE: Conformity to moral rightness in action or attitude; righteousness.

We can all make this declaration; "I have been just and righteous before a Holy God and He has dealt accordingly with me in accordance to his word; Truthfully and Justly. I have received Justice from God who upholds his word."

As we walk uprightly before a holy God then his word will accomplish all that it is designed to do. We do our part and our heavenly Father does his.

The Leah Season looks and sounds something like this…

As he began his journey through the unknown, he came across a distinguished man, tall in stature, one who looked familiar, as though he had seen him somewhere before. He began to speak these words;

"My child, as you begin this walk of purpose, there are some things you should know. There will be days of great contemplation, events will take place that will test you and try you, but fear not when these AFFLICTIONS come, for it is by divine design that they will mold you and shape you into that new creature you are created to be - one that can adapt to the environment using the gifts given to you. It is very important that you rightly HEAR the voice that speaks clearer and more distinct than any other voice you have known. It will call you to a specific place of His choosing. You will become ATTACHED to these words that have been declared over you. You will travel this path through many valleys, many rivers, over the dry lands and the wet lands. You will endure the heat of the day and the darkness of night, but know that you will awake to a morning of CELEBRATION of the manifestation of the words that have been spoken. You will connect with that reality and will be joined with another. You will walk hand in hand as you become familiar with each other. You will be with the one who understands you, the one who knows you, the one that He specifically designed for who you are. I will REWARD you for the times and seasons you will endure, but until that reward comes you will wander far and wide and fight many a battle and ask many questions. It's going to be uncomfortable at times, my child, but I have built you for endurance; I have equipped you with many talents. I know that you can do this.

Look there, upon the horizon. I have prepared a place for you. It has your name written all over it, a perfect fit, specially designed just for you. This is your DWELLING PLACE on the earth. It's beautiful, isn't it? I went to great lengths to make sure every room and every piece of furniture fit exactly who you are. Here are the keys for this place of purpose. Take great care not to lose them; I only made one set and they only fit that one door. There are no duplicates. They are unique, just like you. And by the way, she's waiting inside for you.

My child. My word has been a lamp to your feet and a light to your path. You have walked uprightly before Me and stood the test of time. I have made sure that My word completed everything it was designed to do, even down to the minute details. I have etched an inscription above the doorway of your place. JUSTICE. Well done good and faithful servant. Enter. You have walked into DESTINY. Enjoy!"

Chapter 7

Jacob's Reward

Twenty years had gone by. The Leah Season was now complete and it was Jacob's turn to be transformed into his new identity. He had Rachel by his side, he had stood the test of time and grown in capacity large enough to house his destiny. The package was almost complete and it was time for him to move on. All Jacob had to do was come into total alignment with it. You may be thinking that he already had, but when you go through a Leah Season in life, there is a progressive transformation that changes you from the inside out.

People around you may not immediately notice the change, because it's not physical, it's a change from within. But when you speak, they hear a different sound coming out of your mouth. Throughout life and your walk with God, people have come to know you and see you in a certain way, but now its different. They have either observed you a certain way or associated you with particular activities, traits, successes or failures. Some appreciate you, others don't understand you, but everyone has an opinion about you. However, the greatest manifestation of this is when you begin to believe and witness this change in your own life. There is a new voice, a distinct declaration and a laser-like focus toward the finish line. This is the new identity that is available to every believer when they embrace their destiny.

When we enter into a relationship with the Lord, we put on His identity as a new creature in Christ. Notice in the scripture below where it says, "all things have become new." Other translations say, "a new life has begun." The journey begins with His mark on your life and advances you to a place where you become fully identified with who God has called you to be. In other words, if we don't see ourselves the way God sees us, we will never fully embrace what He has established for our lives.

"Therefore, if anyone is in Christ, he is a new creation; old things have passed away; behold, all things have become new." 2 Corinthians 5:17 (NKJV)

Take Moses for example; when he returned to Egypt after being in the desert for many years, he returned a different man with a new identity. The same applied to Joseph - when he appeared before his brothers in Egypt, they didn't recognize him because of his position and the new identity he had taken.

IT'S TIME TO SAY GOODBYE!

Jacob knew his season with Laban had come to a close. He had lived under another man's roof, or as we will call it, another man's vision, for 20 years. He had served with honor. He had performed his duties with excellence and above all, he had been obedient to Laban's requests. It was now time for him to move on. The stirring within Jacob was nothing more than God giving him the divine push to move into the greater arena of influence that He had originally spoken to him at Bethel.

Now it came about when Rachel had borne Joseph, that Jacob said to Laban, "Send me away, that I may go to my own place and to my own country. "Give me my wives and my children for whom I have served you, and let me

depart; for you yourself know my service which I have rendered you."
Gen. 30:25-26 (NASB)

There is an uncomfortable and disconnected feeling that comes upon you when its time to leave the place where you have been for so many years. It's not that people don't appreciate you anymore or see you as a lesser person, but there is a sense, in God, that there is no more room at the inn. You're not being ousted, rejected or maligned; it's God doing His thing. The nudging of the Holy Spirit is unmistakable, especially when you have felt Him before in other seasons. You just know His touch. It is difficult to describe in words because it comes more as a feeling and a stirring within you, and the only words that can closely express these feelings are ones of being 'out-of-the-loop', 'you don't fit anymore', almost claustrophobic in nature. You know it's time to go.

'I am the Goa of Bethel, where you anointed a pillar, where you made a vow to Me; now arise, leave this land, and return to the land of your birth." Gen. 31:13 (NASB)

It is important during these tender moments that we don't allow an attitude of pride or resentment to enter our thought life. When you are moving into the purpose and plan of God you will find that a small part of you wants to stay behind and the rest of you can't wait to leave. Don't be shocked when people treat you differently or have difficulty figuring you out. They really do not understand what is inside of you and what is transforming in your life by the hand of God.

As Jacob made the journey back to the land of his birth he was impacted with a plethora of emotions, as he knew an encounter with Esau awaited him. He made his petition known before God and repeated the word of the Lord back to Him, just in case He had forgotten what He'd said. I found myself doing the very same thing when I was faced with a difficult situation - relaying back to God what He had said over my life. I'm sure you have done exactly the same. We know God never forgets what He says; it just makes us feel better when we remind Him.

Jacob said, "O God of my father Abraham and God of my father Isaac, O LORD, who said to me, 'Return to your country and to your relatives, and I will prosper you,' I am unworthy of all the loving-kindness and of all the faithfulness which You have shown to Your servant; for with my staff only I crossed this Jordan, and now I have become two companies. "Deliver me, I pray, from the hand of my brother, from the hand of Esau; for I fear him, that he will come and attack me ana the mothers with the children. "For You said, 'I will surely prosper you and make your descendants as the sand of the sea, which is too great to be numbered.'" Gen. 32:9-12 (NASB)

Jacob was no doubt having flashbacks from 20 years ago and the unrest he had left at home. Was he about to face an angry brother and an army of 400 men? Would he lose everything he had worked so hard to build - his family, Leah and Rachel? Only time would tell and the only assurance that Jacob had was the word of the Lord.

Can you trust God's word in the face of adversity when the circumstances paint a differing view of what God said?

Chapters 32 and 33 of Genesis provide incredible examples of divine intervention for Jacob, (Israel) and Esau and take us to the place where Jacob was totally engaged with who he was and what God had called him to do. Prior to his encounter with God, Jacob sent forth a multitude of gifts to Esau, no doubt an attempt to appease his brother (Gen. 32:20 NASB). After gathering his family and possessions together and leading them across the Jabbok River, he remained alone in the camp overnight where he wrestled with God until daybreak.

64

Then Jacob was left alone, and a man wrestled with him until daybreak. When he saw that he had not prevailed against him, he touched the socket of his thigh; so the socket of Jacob's thigh was dislocated while he wrestled with him. Then he said, "Let me go, for the dawn is breaking." But he said, "I will not let you go unless you bless me." So he said to him, "What is your name?" And he said, "Jacob." He said, "Your name shall no longer be Jacob, but Israel; for you have striven with God and with men and have prevailed.' Gen 32:24-28 (NASB)

COUNTING THE COST

Anyone who walks with God in preparation for his or her destiny has a limp just like Jacob's. Not all are physical marks, but many represent the dealings of God that are embedded deep within a person's life. As we have discussed in previous chapters, your walk with God will cost you something. It has a price attached to it, not for your harm, but for the glory of God and His purpose for your life.

Even from a practical standpoint, anyone wishing to accomplish a certain goal must work towards that end result. It will cost them something to achieve and succeed. It's the same principle with God. The difference being that He has equipped you to further His Kingdom and not your own, to declare His word and influence the environment where He has positioned you for His glory. You will have the battle scars to prove you have been in a fight - proof of resilience in times of struggle, faith in the times of uncertainty, trust in the times of disappointment and dependency in the times of solitude. It is a battle, let's not forget that, but the proven warrior takes the high ground and conquers the mountain he has been assigned.

The first time Jacob had an encounter with God was when he was running from Esau and for his life. He had no idea of who he was or where he was going until God imparted a word that set a specific course of action into motion. The second time he encountered God was returning back to the place of his birth to face his brother, now as a man of purpose and destiny. He wasn't running anymore. Jacob's Leah Season had been completed and now as Israel, he knew who he was in God's ultimate plan for his life.

Something happened to Jacob in the wrestling of God that not only transformed his identity from the inside out, but also affected the spiritual atmosphere over a nation. This was evident when he came face to face with Esau.

But he himself passed on ahead of them and bowed down to the ground seven times, until he came near to his brother. Then Esau ran to meet him and embraced him, and fell on his neck and kissed him, and they wept. Gen. 33:3-4 (NASB)

No matter what it is that God has planned for your future, and whatever pathway you take, when you arrive at the place where you understand and see the completed you in the framework of God, it will be as if heaven connected with earth in a resounding applause where past, present and future collided for such a time as this.

Take the time to allow God to do what he needs to do in your life and you will surely see the fulfillment of your destiny.

CONCLUSION

FIGHT THE GOOD FIGHT

You have just read an account of a man named Jacob and his two wives, Leah and Rachel. Their story will remain forever written in the scriptures for those who care to read it. Some will call it a love story; some simply see it as a guy who had two wives. For those of you who have just taken the time to read this account, you can see it as a journey towards destiny.

My question for you is this: Will the life you live from this moment forward be written down on the pages of a book, inscribed on the hearts of those you have influenced or affect generations to come? Whether you are called to business, politics, ministry, family, media, arts, education or any other field of influence, God has positioned you to make a difference. He has equipped and gifted you for a specific responsibility. You will be tested and challenged, you will want to give up, you will be criticized and misunderstood, but when the dust settles, you will come out of the refiner's fire as pure gold with destiny in your hands.

My life's story is woven throughout the pages of this book, and as you read about Jacob and his struggles along his journey to destiny you read about mine. Your life is also written within these pages and only you can identify what specific chapter you're in. You may not be called to change a nation but you are called to make a difference in the lives of those you come in contact with. You will accomplish all that God has assigned for you.

Your life is a tapestry. Every stitch and every precise movement of the crafter's needle is designed with purpose in mind, to create a portrait of a finished work that has already been established in the heavens. You are a finished work in God's eyes and He knows the path you are to take, so trust Him with your life.

God knows the very breath you breathe. He knows the exact details of your life and what it will take for you to embrace your destiny in Him. Don't allow the disappointments and frustrations to abort that purpose. No matter what unforeseen events take place, no matter the struggle, keep your eyes fixed on the author and finisher of your faith.

It's what you will birth in this season that allows you to truly embrace your destiny in God. This season, the Leah Season, holds truths that are not immediately revealed but over time will become very evident as you see every piece come together. Without the Leah Season, you will not be able to utter these words:

I have fought the good fight, I have finished the course, I have kept the faith; 2 Timothy 4:7 (NASB)

ACKNOWLEDGEMENTS

TO MY DEAR WIFE SHARON;

For believing in me and supporting me through this book. Your patience, strength and encouragement made all the difference.

TO THE GREAT LEADERS IN MY LIFE;

Rev. Al & Joyce Dovidio, Rev. Mary L. Edlin. Thank you for your encouraging words and great wisdom, you are forever faithful and pillars in the Kingdom.

TO AINSLEY, JOHN-WESLEY AND MICHAEL.

You are a great treasure in a father's heart. Thank you for believing in me when I didn't believe in myself. Thank you for following after God. You make a father very proud.

TO THE LEAH SEASON, YOU TAUGHT ME A LOT.

Without the difficult times and deep struggles, I would have never known the purpose for your existence.

TO THE LORD MY GOD;

Your word will not return void. It will accomplish what it was designed to do.

ABOUT THE AUTHOR

Rev. Paul Barratt has lived in the United States with his family for three decades. After leaving his home country, England, he and his wife began a journey that would span over 30 years.

His passion for the pursuit of God led him and his family to many different places and diverse encounters with seasons that would define their purpose and calling in God.

After an encounter with God in 1999, Paul's life changed in a direction he did not expect. There was a great dissatisfaction that came over him and his desire to seek more of God grew even deeper. Knowing that God was stirring his heart, in 2002, he and his family traveled across country to a remote place in the Rocky Mountains of Colorado. It was here, through a 7-year period of time, that the hand of God molded and shaped them. There were good days and there were ugly days but God was doing a work that would span multiple generations.

"There must be more to life than going to work every week and attending church twice a week, there has to be a specific purpose!"

This statement would resound in his hearing for many years as his quest to find destiny resulted in a roller coaster ride of disappointments and appointments, failures and favor setbacks and set-ups. But he and his wife never stopped believing that God had placed within them certain gifts and talents to be used specifically for their destiny.

DESTINY was written out of this journey. It has propelled Paul to become an author and communicator to the Body of Christ, to speak of his own personal journey and also help others identify their own purpose and destiny for their lives.

There is a dream inside every person and a voice crying out to be heard. You were designed for destiny and you are the administrator to the great architect of heaven and earth, the Lord God Almighty.

It is Paul's desire to see individuals reach their God given Destiny. There is no greater fulfillment than to succeed in the things of God and see that change affect every aspect of your environment, culture and the community were you live.

62041826R00042

Made in the USA
Middletown, DE
18 January 2018